THE FISH HAWK
OSPREY

D1025519

Acknowledgments

Even after a lifetime of wildlife study, observation and appreciation, no individual can honestly claim to know and to have seen it all, and so the most complete guidebook is one in which many have contributed their knowledge and experience.

Personal observation is the key to presenting a diverse picture of any wild creature, and some of those who have helped me paint my osprey portrait include: Larry Rymon, East Stroudsburg University; Pat Corr, head of Maine's waterfowl research program; Alan Hutchinson, Maine's Endangered and Non-Game project leader; Daniel Brauning, Pennsylvania Game Commission wildlife biologist; David Loveland, International Osprey Foundation; Anne James, Cornell University Laboratory of Ornithology; Allison McCollough of Etna, Maine; and Becky and Stanley Thompson of Powder Springs, Georgia.

Thanks also to librarians Maria Armitage and Michelle Johnson; and Barbara Harold, NorthWord Press, Inc. Managing Editor, for her guidance and direction.

© Stephen D. Carpenteri, 1997

Photography © 1997: Charles H. Willey, 30, 36-37, 48-49, 92-93, 94-95, 113; Robert Lankinen/The Wildlife Collection, 1, 33; Tom Vezo, Front cover, 4-5, 8, 12, 14-15, 19, 23, 24-25, 28-29, 87, 88-89, 111, 122-123; Bob & Clara Calhoun/Bruce Coleman, Inc., 6-7; Tom & Pat Leeson, 10-11, 44-45, 78, 96-97, 132-133; Arthur Morris/BIRDS AS ART, 16, 35, 46, 124-125, Back cover; Richard Day/Daybreak Imagery, 20, 65, 114-115; John Shaw/Bruce Coleman, Inc., 26, 40; Fritz Polking/Dembinsky Photo Associates, 38-39, 53, 54, 61, 118-119, 128-129, 134; Joe McDonald/Bruce Coleman, Inc., 42-43, 62-63, 98; D. Robert Franz/The Wildlife Collection, 50, 56-57; Rick Poley, 58, 72-73; Jock Montgomery/Bruce Coleman, Inc., 66; Larry Minden/Minden Pictures, 68-69; Clay Myers/The Wildlife Collection, 70, 74, 76-77; John Giustina/The Wildlife Collection, 80-81; Bill Lea/Dembinsky Photo Associates, 82; Stan Osolinski/Dembinsky Photo Associates, 85, 120; Dominique Braud/Dembinsky Photo Associates, 91, 100-101; Susan Day/Daybreak Imagery, 102-103; Joanne Williams/BIRDS AS ART, 105; Tom Vezo/The Wildlife Collection, 106, 126-127; Bill Lea, 108-109, 130; Jeff Foott/ Bruce Coleman, Inc., 116.

NorthWord Press
5900 Green Oak Drive
Minnetonka, Minnesota 55343
1-800-328-3895

Book design by Kenneth Hey

Library of Congress Cataloging-in-Publication Data
Carpenteri, Stephen.
      Osprey : the fish hawk / by Stephen D. Carpenteri.
          p. cm. — (NorthWord wildlife series)
       ISBN 1-55971-590-1 (sc)
    1. Osprey. 2. Osprey—North America. I. Title. II. Series.
    QL696.F36C37 1997
    598.9'3–dc21   96-46821

Printed in Singapore

THE FISH HAWK
OSPREY

by Stephen D. Carpenteri

NORTHWORD®

NORTHWORD PRESS
Minnetonka, Minnesota

Dedication

For Karen Anne, Kody and Brad

Contents

Introduction   9

Chapter 1   The Fish Hawk   17

Chapter 2   Airborne Angler   31

Chapter 3   Osprey Ways   51

Chapter 4   At Home and Away   79

Chapter 5   Threats to Osprey Survival   99

Chapter 6   Ospreys and You   121

             Further Reading   135

Introduction

Prior to the 1950s, ospreys were lumped with all other birds of prey under one less-than-flattering heading—vermin. At that time, it was acceptable for U.S. farmers, hunters, and bird- and fish-hatchery operators to kill any and all such winged predators caught in the act of (or en route to) game or stock depredation. The practice was (and is) common worldwide as well. In the United States, a form of this law still pertains to crows, although it has not been explained how one determines that a flying crow is "about to commit depredations" on crops or livestock!

The indiscriminate killing of raptors was not always considered by the public to be a threat to the longevity of these species, but a study conducted in Great Britain in the 1950s forever changed the thinking of Americans regarding the value and place of birds of prey in the ecosystem (a term that was not even coined until decades later). In that study, a long-term decline in raptor numbers in western Europe was traced to high levels of common pesticides, notably DDT, in the eggshells of avian predators. Further study revealed that the various pesticides in common use at the time by farmers, orchardists, silviculturists and other agricultural interests were severely affecting

A female osprey waits for her mate to deliver the next meal.

Previous pages: A courting male osprey presents
a freshly caught fish to a prospective mate.

the reproductive physiology of female raptors, including ospreys. These studies determined that pesticide contamination often resulted in either missing or broken eggs. In addition, high levels of synthetic chemicals were found in the eggs, organs and fatty tissue of many adult raptors, sometimes in fatal quantities.

The most threatening effect of pesticide poisoning in predatory birds involved the chemicals' effects on the birds' reproductive processes. In simple terms, ingestion of DDT and other synthetic chemicals causes disruptions in the female's ability to produce calcium, which is vital for the production of eggshells. When eggshells are produced that cannot support the weight of the incubating parent, the shells may crack or break. Also, a lack of sufficient calcium in the eggshell may affect bone growth in the developing chick embryo. Because most raptors, particularly ospreys, will re-nest only once, or occasionally twice, after the initial nesting attempt fails, it is easy to see how egg loss can severely affect a colony of ospreys over time, even when the health of the adult bird is not directly at risk due to chemical contamination.

In 1972, the chemical DDT was banned. In most areas, immediate positive results were observed. The same year, protection of all North American Falconiformes was accomplished through state, federal, provincial and Canadian laws, which made it illegal to kill, own or possess predatory birds, their parts, eggs or nests. By 1984, ospreys were ranked near last on the list of raptors deemed most vulnerable to extirpation or extinction due to chemical contamination or poaching in the United States.

As might be expected, decimation of osprey and other raptor populations via pesticide contamination occurred most noticeably in areas with heavy industrial or agricultural activity, while in true wilderness areas, the effects of chemical poisoning was statistically less.

When not actively fishing, ospreys spend their time perched on exposed limbs near the nest.

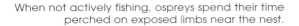

Environmental pollution and the threat of a "silent spring" became the rallying point through the 1980s, and while the battle for clean air, soil and water will never end, large predatory birds like the osprey have clearly benefited from the removal of chemical contaminants from the environment.

More good news for U.S. osprey populations came about in 1979, when biologist Larry Rymon of East Stroudsburg University in Pennsylvania tried "hacking," or reintroducing osprey young, to their former Keystone State haunts. Starting with just six chicks, Rymon successfully returned some 110 ospreys to the Pocono Mountain region. "Ours were the first ospreys hacked in the United States that returned to their natal nest sites," Rymon notes. "By 1985, the first hacked osprey nest was built, and the first young were produced. Our birds came back to thrive in areas of the state where they had been extirpated by DDT/DDE poisoning and random shooting in the decades before our hacking project began."

Since Rymon's initial, ground-breaking project, at least twelve other states have instituted osprey hacking projects, with Kansas and Ohio joining the fold in 1996. Over 1,000 ospreys have been successfully hacked, and 120 new nests have been built and used by paired hacked birds.

It is no surprise that serious osprey study began only after the species was nearly extirpated in the United States by unregulated pesticide use. As is too often the case, near disaster breeds direct action, but the osprey was the lucky one in this scenario. It wasn't until scientists began to live with and study the osprey that they learned how adaptable and resilient this hardy, long-distance migrant really is. The information derived from over thirty years of intense osprey study has been the basis for the hugely successful hacking and nest-site enhancement projects that have been conducted in the United States and other countries in recent years.

This is not, then, a book lamenting the decline of another species in the twentieth century due to human error. Instead, it is a celebration of the successful rejuvenation of a species that, a generation after being declared on the brink of extinction, is now the most common of all the world's winged predators. With so many other species teetering on endangered or threatened lists throughout the modern world, the osprey is one that still gives all naturalists, novice and expert alike, something to smile about as we enter the twenty-first century.

The M-shaped wing formation and dark-feathered "wrist" patch are tell-tale signs of an osprey on the wing.

Following pages: A fierce looking predator, the osprey is actually docile and sociable within the colony.

Chapter
One

The Fish Hawk

I t is one of the ironies of nature that our most common bird of prey is invariably mistaken for some other winged predator. The irony is that, for about twelve million years, the osprey has been in a taxonomic class of its own. In fact, no other bird of prey is really quite like it.

Although osprey populations are well established throughout the world, their habitat choice keeps them out of the eye of the general public. Creatures of the lakes, rivers, bays and coastal marshes, ospreys are the only "pure" fish-eaters among the raptors, thus giving them their nickname. Being so, they are rarely seen far from water. Their large size, hooked beak and soaring flight patterns lead untrained observers to shout, "Look, an eagle!" Many who research no further go away convinced that a bald or golden eagle is what they've been privileged to see.

Evolution

Taxonomists have yet to sort out all of the differences between ospreys, hawks, owls, eagles and other raptors, but most agree that there is no evidence

An efficient angler, the osprey enjoys one of the highest catch rates of all raptors.

available on the existence of ospreys prior to the Pleistocene, or Ice Age. Our only fish-eating, dive-into-the-water hawk, some time in the last twelve million years or so the osprey plunged into its present niche as a fish-eating, migratory predator, earning it the coveted "cosmopolitan" rating reserved only for common, prolific species found essentially everywhere their preferred habitat exists.

Four osprey subspecies have been recognized by scientists: *Pandion haliaetus carolinsis* (the North American variety), *P. h. haliaetus* (European, northeast coast of Africa, and Asia north of the Himalayas), *P. h. ridgwayi* (Caribbean), and *P. h. cryostats* (Australia, New Guinea and nearby South Pacific islands).

In the northern hemisphere, ospreys have been common for somewhere between ten and fifteen million years. Vague fossilized specimens from the mid-Miocene era (thirteen million years ago) have been suggested as being osprey related. Biologist Alan Poole romanticizes with the notion that ospreys may have played an integral part in the culture and myths of Ice Age Cro Magnon and Neandertal peoples.

What's in a Name

Although the Greek name "haliaetus" means, literally, "sea eagle," the term is misleading. The osprey is related more to hawks than to eagles. The North American osprey's full scientific name is loosely translated to mean "bone-breaking sea eagle."

Taxonomists remain divided on the *Pandion haliaetus* moniker, which was bestowed on the osprey by British taxonomist Lesson in 1828. Problems among language experts with the literal interpretation of the antics of the mythical being Pandion (in which intra-family intrigue ends with two errant sisters being changed into a swallow and a nightingale, to be chased forever by a conniving husband's hawk) led taxonomists to include the osprey in the order Falconiformes (which includes hawks and falcons); and more recently within the suborder Accipitridae. Part of the reason for this change includes subtle variations in skeletal, musculature and feather formation.

In the 1920s, the taxonomic dust storm cleared when *Pandion* had been reduced to one species composed of the four races of ospreys now accepted by taxonomists worldwide. Since then, small rumblings of "new" ospreys have been heard, but none have been credited with authenticity—yet.

The dark eye band and white breast identifies this as an adult male osprey.

New strides in biochemical research techniques are helping scientists further unravel the mysteries of osprey evolution, and ongoing studies may soon clear up some of the muddied waters that presently exist in raptorial taxonomy. For now, however, it is safe to say that ospreys, due primarily to their singular feeding and migration habits, are definitely in a class of their own.

Physical Characteristics

It is no wonder that ospreys are often mistaken by the untrained observer for eagles. Nearly two feet in length at maturity, ospreys have a wingspan approaching six feet. On takeoff from the nest or a tree branch, the osprey's widespread wings are held in a distinctive "M" shape when observed from below. The "M" ("bent at the elbows") shape of the osprey's wing silhouette is in contrast to the eagle's "+" ("straight across") wing silhouette while in flight; and is thus one way to distinguish between the two while in flight.

In the soft, unshadowed light of dawn or dusk, the osprey's dark brown upper body has a faint tinge of purple that few photos or artist's renderings can adequately capture. The osprey's underparts are white, with a paler brown lower throat and breast. The crown of the head and nape of the neck are buff-colored and darkly streaked. Separating the nape from the white throat is a distinctive broad, dark stripe that runs from the front of the head back through the bright yellow eye (in adults) to the shoulder. The osprey's underparts appear pure white in flight, with distinctive barring visible on the underwings and tail. The average weight of an adult osprey is 3 to 4-1/2 pounds.

The osprey has a dark crest on its head, but does not erect it in the manner of cardinals, waxwings or jays. Instead, the osprey's crest rides up in the wind like the loose feathers of Robin Hood's cap.

The osprey's wings are "fingered" at the ends in flight, and display a striking, identifying dark patch of feathers at the "wrist." Because no American eagle has a white underbody or dark-feathered wrist, birders of experience can distinguish the difference between ospreys and eagles at a glance. In fact, only the black-shouldered kite, a smaller bird of prey restricted to western and southern states, even remotely resembles the osprey in flight coloration.

Unlike most other water-based birds, notably waterfowl, ospreys gradually molt a few feathers at a time so they are able to hunt and migrate without interruption. The molting process stops just prior to migration and,

Strong wings enable the osprey to cover more territory while hunting.

for males, during the breeding season, as it is the males that are responsible for the bulk of the feeding of their mates and young. Some ospreys have been reported that have white feathers replacing dark ones, but this is a rarity in the species.

The osprey lacks the distinctive supraorbital ridge over the eye which gives most other birds of prey their trademark "angry" look. The osprey does, however, have a ridge of dark feathers over the eye that biologists believe may serve to reduce the glare while hunting over sunlit waters. The color of an immature osprey's iris is red to orange, changing to bright yellow in adulthood. Like most other raptors, the osprey's eyesight is eight times greater than humans'.

The osprey's cere, or nostril area, and legs are a dull blue-gray, while its hooked beak and sharp talons are black. The talons grow continuously, and must be worn down by regular use, much as a beaver's incisors will continue to grow if not kept short and sharp by frequent gnawing.

The osprey's preening gland located at the base of the tail secretes a pungent oil that will linger in the bird's plumage for decades, often remaining on the feathered carcasses of laboratory study specimens despite years of storage. The osprey's plumage is dense and oily in order to resist saturation, but repeated exposure to water will soak them eventually, rendering the birds temporarily flightless, a condition that can be a threat to survival under some conditions—such as when prolonged, severe storms coincide with the spring nesting season.

Female ospreys have short streaks of color in the breast feathers that form a mottled "necklace" rarely seen, or which is poorly developed, in males. Immature ospreys have a noticeable scaly appearance on their back feathers, which is due to white- or light-colored edging on the back and upper wing covers.

Ospreys in tropical and subtropical climates are generally smaller than their northern counterparts, a phenomenon observed in other species as well. Subtle differences in feather color exists among subspecies, but, as a rule, all ospreys look alike except under very close scrutiny.

Dimorphism, in which females weigh more or are larger than males, is exhibited in all four ospreys subspecies. Longer wings, tails, talons and bills are evident, although it is uncertain why, because it is the male that does the bulk of the hunting for the family, as well as most of the chasing of intruders.

The osprey's dark eye band may help reduce glare while gliding over sunlit waters.

It may be that the female, during breeding and nesting, simply does less flying and more eating, and thereby has the time and protein input necessary for enhanced development, but the ornithological jury is still out on this subject.

When perched, ospreys appear long-legged and bent over, or "hunched," with wingtips extending just beyond the tail tip. Ospreys leave the nest or perch on widespread wings, and in flight exhibit slow, steady, shallow wingbeats. Ospreys soar and glide with wings crooked, wrists cocked forward and held above body level, and the wingtips are pointed down and back. Ospreys will sometimes soar on flat wings, eagle fashion, but only the osprey halts and hovers over water on beating wings.

When perched on the nest or on a limb near its favorite hunting grounds, the osprey appears dark brown above and white below. Rather than assuming the ramrod-straight, vertical attitude of most perched hawks and owls, the osprey at rest often appears gangly and disheveled, with no hint of the grace and fluidity it exhibits in flight.

Identifying an osprey at a distance, especially over water, is simply a matter of watching and waiting for the bird to exhibit its trademark hover-and-plunge behavior. While actively hunting, the osprey is our only raptor that will stop, wings aflutter like some giant butterfly, over water. At this point, the bird is

In flight, the osprey exhibits slow, shallow wingbeats.

searching for fish suspended within the bird's optimum striking depth of three feet or less. The osprey may abort several dives before finally plunging in to strike, but it is this distinctive feeding behavior that distinguishes the osprey from all other winged predators. In fact, many experienced birders reserve making their identification of distant, water-habitat Falconiformes until they've seen whether or not the subject enters the telltale hovering mode that can only mean a hunting osprey.

Generally speaking, if a hawk-like bird swoops low over a bar, river or marsh without hovering, odds are it's something other than an osprey. An exception to this rule is when an osprey has already made a successful dive, in which case it will be easy to see the bird's quarry clutched tightly in its talons, headfirst, as the bird flies low over the water, back to its nest or perch to feed.

In time, as more people come to know and understand the nuances of identifying and appreciating these marvelous, impressive birds of prey, the day may come when everyone who sees them will shout, "That's an osprey!"

When perched, the osprey appears hunched
and somewhat "raggedy" compared to other raptors.

Following pages: Osprey field marks include a white underside
and distinctively barred underwings.

Chapter Two

Airborne Angler

T he osprey goes about the business of catching fish with a skill and accuracy unmatched among the world's predatory birds. In North America, the osprey has shown a phenomenal 90 percent success rate in some catches-per-dive studies, with a nationwide average of nearly 40 percent—well above the catch rates of most eagles, hawks and owls.

What's for Dinner?

Because ospreys do not require a single species of prey to survive, they are able to set up housekeeping wherever shallow-water fish species can be found. In many cases, ospreys seem to prefer slow-moving, bottom-feeding, shallows-dwelling species such as suckers, bullheads, catfish, carp, fallfish, flounder, perch and sunfish; but they may also take eels, trout, bass, pike and pickerel, as well as other free-swimming or schooling species that forage or travel near the water's surface.

Herring and menhaden, especially, appear at the water's surface in large schools in the osprey's preferred estuarine habitat, offering easy pickings to

After a catch, ospreys turn their prey headfirst for smoother flight.

ospreys that nest on the Atlantic Coast. Herring also offer abundant opportunities as they migrate into coastal streams to spawn. When these schools move on, ospreys will return to hunting other localized species.

Inland ospreys may eat the same species all season, while coastal birds tend to change their diet as local prey abundance and variety fluctuates due to seasonal or migrational patterns. When feeding on migratory species such as mullet or shad, ospreys seem to prefer fish that are fat and healthy over spawned-out specimens, abandoning one post-spawn species in favor of the next, roe-rich migrants.

The average osprey weighs less than 4 pounds, and can take fish of equal size, although fish weighing 14 to 22 ounces is about the average size catch preferred by adult ospreys.

Benthic (bottom feeding) fish are easier for ospreys to catch than piscavorous (predatory) species, as the latter are quicker and more likely to utilize nearby surface cover such as rocks, logs and other structures for protection. In the final analysis, it is depth, not species, that seems to be the critical and deciding factor in what ospreys eat. Any fish that is in water deeper than three feet is essentially safe from the osprey's sharp talons.

In some studies, individual ospreys did show a distinct preference for a particular prey species, but in most cases it was the presence of captive quarry (stocked lakes, ponds or hatchery pools) that influenced their choice. If an osprey is offered the opportunity to feed on hatchery trout, bass or salmon, it would seem only reasonable that it would continue to take the free and easy meal over having to work harder for its dinner. Like any other predator, the osprey will not waste its time on prey it cannot easily catch, as the caloric loss would be too costly to recover.

Adding to the osprey's broad range of forage is the fact that fish don't even have to be on the menu, or at least not always. Ospreys have occasionally displayed a taste for carrion, rodents, small birds, turtles, frogs and crustaceans, although these incidental kills rarely comprise more than 2 percent of the bird's diet.

The question of ospreys eating species other than fish is still a matter of debate among researchers, because ospreys readily scavenge birds and mammal carcasses for use as nesting material. Simply seeing an osprey with a vole, squirrel or bird in its talons is not sufficient evidence to proclaim that ospreys often and readily eat such prey, although it is probably safe to say

The osprey prefers to dine at the nest or on a nearby perch.

that some ospreys, under certain conditions, will eat things other than fish, at least sporadically. In addition, while ospreys have been observed scavenging dead or dying fish on occasion, experts agree that 98 percent or more of their diet consists of live, fresh-caught fish.

The Hunt Begins

In nearly all cases, the osprey finds and feeds on its prey near or over water. There have been few observations recorded of ospreys hunting and feeding widely over land in the manner of hawks, owls and falcons, although some instances of such behavior have been cited. As with every other living species, individual ospreys sometimes do things not normally associated with the behavior of the main population, and so there will be exceptions to every osprey rule.

The osprey is our only bird of prey that actually dives into the water to catch its prey. Other winged, fish-eating predators, notably the bald eagle, swoop down to skim the water, reach out and snatch prey from the surface, but the osprey rarely exhibits such behavior. Almost without exception, the osprey plops headlong into the water to snatch its prey. However, when hunting small or fast-moving fish such as sardines or shad, the osprey may hunt or hover at lower-than-normal altitudes, snatching fish right off the surface in the manner normally associated with eagles.

Ospreys spend most of their time between feedings perched on a limb over the water, or at the nest, preening droop-winged, sometimes fluffing and shaking to dry themselves off prior to the next hunt. While resting they may stretch their wings and legs in an awkward-looking fashion. When it is time to hunt, usually during the period from mid morning to late afternoon, the osprey leaves its roost on widespread wings, feet tucked beneath its tail. The serious business of fishing is underway, and there is no more effective winged angler than the osprey.

All Wings and Eyes

Soaring out over the water at an average altitude of between fifty and a hundred feet, the osprey watches the shallows for prey to appear. When a fish is spotted, the osprey hovers overhead, tail spread, wings fanning rapidly, as the bird jockeys for precise position over its target.

Ospreys are constantly soaring, halting, hovering, backing and circling while hunting, all apparently part of the seek–find–commit sequence that constitutes a successful hunt. When a dive is imminent, the osprey pulls its wings back and free-falls to the water, feet outstretched, using its wings and

Ospreys constantly soar, backing and circling, while they hunt.

tail intermittently to adjust its fall and to stay on target.

Many times the osprey will make a halting, lilting preliminary dive, as if to make certain in midair that the target is indeed a fish of the proper size. Some dives are aborted at the last instant as the bird realizes that it cannot complete its attack, or that, for some other reason, it decides to turn away from its prey.

The Plunge

When the osprey commits to a dive, it plunges downward with head and feet held nearly together, as if the bird were sighting over its toes to ensure the accuracy of its fall.

Most dives are made from about 65 to 100 feet above the water, at angles ranging from 45 degrees to nearly vertical. Some ospreys have been observed diving from a height of 230 feet, and from as close as about 16 feet, but such variations are often caused by unusual conditions or situations that the osprey is merely adjusting to. An osprey may repeat the soar–hover sequence a dozen times between dives, a process that can take the bird far up or down-stream within its home territory—as far as sixteen miles away from the nest in one New England study. Generally, hunting forays rarely take the osprey into the territory of another nesting pair, and the average adult osprey will spend just twelve to twenty minutes between catches, although fledglings may spend more time refining their novice techniques.

Following pages: Occasionally ospreys snatch prey from the surface, in the manner of eagles and other fish-eaters.

The Catch

An osprey usually disappears under the water after a spectacular, plunging dive, reaching with outstretched talons for its prey, but the bird may simply dimple the surface as it grabs for a fish. Several seconds may pass as the bird completes its plunge, and it is at this point that the osprey's specially developed feet come into play.

When a fish is caught, the bird rests briefly on the water, latching securely onto its struggling prey, before reaching high out of the water with its wings to become airborne. Using its double-jointed front toe with its rear toes, the osprey arranges its catch as it flies so that the fish is held head-first, torpedo-like, to reduce wind resistance while en route to the perch or nest.

The osprey's toes are equal in length, and are positioned in a distinctive cross formation as it reaches for its victim. The pads beneath the osprey's toes are covered with sharp, spiny scales, allowing the bird to grip slippery fish with ease. The osprey's talons are long, sharp and rounded, not grooved as in other birds of prey. This allows the osprey to quickly

Ospreys generally do not take fish larger than they can safely handle in flight.

sink its talons into wet, struggling fish. Osprey feet snap shut in .002 of a second, plenty fast enough to catch and hold the quickest fish! The bird's outer toe works in concert with its rear toe to grasp, hold and arrange captured prey.

The osprey's nostrils are unusually long and slitted and may be closed during dives. The bird's feathers are thick and compact, which reduces the threat of waterlogging, although ospreys can sink below the surface and drown if they remain in the water for long periods of time.

Initially, caught fish are held as captured—backward, sideways, or even dangling by the head or tail. Some ospreys have been observed "swimming" after a dive, perhaps to take time to handle or recapture struggling prey. Some birds have even drowned when fish too large were snared and could not be released quickly enough to prevent the osprey from being dragged under.

After the Catch

Ospreys usually fly low over the water after a successful dive, apparently in order to avoid crosswinds or heavy gusts. They also shiver off excess water while en route to the nest or perch.

Occasionally, as the osprey flies off with its prey, another fish-eating bird (usually an eagle) will attempt to steal the osprey's catch in midair. Usually, only birds larger than the osprey will attempt such a move, although, rarely, smaller hawks, gulls and even other ospreys will play the thief, albeit unsuccessfully.

While the diving plunge is the osprey's foraging trademark, observers have reported all variations of diving, stooping or skimming behavior in these birds. In one study, for example, an osprey was observed dragging its feet for long distances across the surface of the water, and when fish began jumping or dodging aside, the osprey would seize its prey without resorting to the standard hover–plunge sequence.

Observers have also reported seeing ospreys make any number of multiple catches, including two fish in one talon, one fish in each talon, and even double catches with both feet! Of course, such events are generally reflective of a very high abundance of fish, and at such times thievery by other fish-eaters is more likely, and often more successful.

After making a catch, this osprey has paused to rest and dry out before feeding.

Following pages: Ospreys often have to protect their catch from scavengers.

When the osprey returns to its perch to begin feeding, it waits for its prey to die; then it uses its strong, tough beak to tear off pieces of skin and flesh, usually starting with the head. When eating, ospreys tear off small chunks of fish, but occasionally swallow whole pieces of skin, bones and other large chunks. They regurgitate pellets of indigestible matter in the same manner as hawks and owls, but most often their food passes normally through the digestive system.

The Search for Food

Although flight burns up much more energy than perching, ospreys generally hunt on the wing, possibly because flight enables them to cover larger areas more effectively than does sitting in one place and watching just the small area beneath the nest or perch. One study, however, disclosed that ospreys in one colony spent about 25 percent of their time hunting from a perch or nest, possibly a reflection on the abundance of prey available at the time.

Wintering ospreys seem to hunt more from a perch than do nesting birds, but biologists believe that this is because non-breeding ospreys have more time and only themselves to feed during this period.

Ospreys normally hunt alone, but they have been observed hunting in groups when the volume of prey allows, such as when large schools of migrating mullet, menhaden, herring or sardines are present.

Ospreys spend as much as 25 percent of their time hunting.

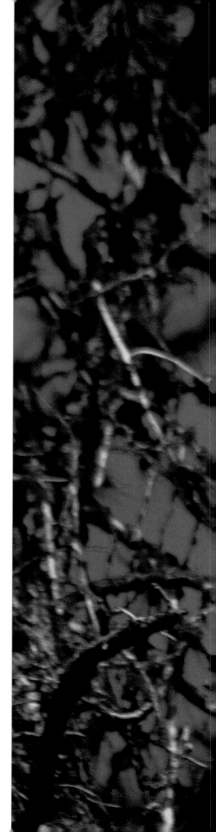

Ospreys target fish by size rather than species.

In addition, most ospreys seem to prefer the same foraging grounds, and will often return to them year after year.

Ospreys apparently communicate the existence of good fishing grounds to other birds in a colony, because observers have reported instances where individual ospreys have returned to the nest with certain, school-species fish, apparently signaling the presence of abundant food to other ospreys in the colony. This causes the other birds to go (with remarkable accuracy) to the same hunting site, even though it may be many miles offshore. Yet, when foraging ospreys return to the nest or perch with hard-to-find species such as flounders, the other birds in the colony are not as likely to get involved with a prolonged search for such difficult-to-find meals.

Ordinary weather conditions such as clouds, rain or gusting winds do not have a great impact on osprey hunting success, but prolonged, severe storms during the nesting season can result in starvation of the young if the adults are not able to forage freely. High winds and muddied waters can also cause ospreys to stop hunting, at least until the unsettled condition passes.

A large part of the reason ospreys are so common worldwide is the otherwise restrictive predator/prey equation. Biologists have long known that predator populations are dependent upon the abundance of prey species. Predator populations can exist at levels no greater than can be supported by the population of their prey. Of course, the habitat and food sources of that prey must be factored in as well. Some avian predatory species, such as the snail-eating kite, are severely limited in range and numbers due to that bird's specialized food source. Ospreys, on the other hand, feed all but exclusively on live fish, a relatively abundant, worldwide food source. So it makes sense that, barring unforeseen disasters on a worldwide scale, the predator/prey equation will ensure that large numbers of ospreys will continue to thrive.

Always creatures of contradictions, ospreys have been observed hovering over water almost 1,000 feet in altitude, following schools of tiny sardines several miles offshore. This behavior is in direct contrast to the osprey's normal habit of hunting close to the water, near shore, for fish in the one-half pound class. It is important to remember that ospreys are adaptable, and will adjust the "rules" of osprey behavior in their own favor as necessary to survive and flourish.

Following pages: After a catch is made, the osprey leaps skyward using the air, not the water, for propulsion.

Chapter
Three

Osprey Ways

O ne of the greatest challenges of wildlife research involves studying individual animal behavior and discovering why a particular stimuli generates a corresponding response. Many are the mysteries involving osprey behavior, and while researchers may never know all of the reasons why ospreys do what they do, biologists have learned much about the everyday life of these remarkable birds.

Vocalizations

While it may be anthropomorphic to suggest that ospreys have their own personalities, it is safe to say that they do tend to react in predictable ways when confronted by various situations. For example, biologist Alan Poole and others have recorded osprey vocalizations in an effort to categorize their utterances and the instances in which they occur. These studies have disclosed that ospreys utter three specific types of calls: guard calls, alarm calls and begging calls. The guard call, a low-key, reserved series of whistled notes that vary in intensity as danger or an intruder draws near, is not necessarily a

Ospreys are all business when it comes to feeding
and defending their families.

warning of impending danger, but seems to be more of an indicator that the osprey knows trouble is imminent and wants no part of it.

Alarm calls are clear *"tchip"* notes uttered in varying pitch, sequence and intensity, but they are always uttered when an intruder crosses that invisible line between "in the area" and "too close for comfort." When serious trouble arises, perhaps when a marauding raccoon or owl is lurking nearby, an entire colony of ospreys may join in uttering the alarm call, a cacophonous sound which is certain to drive the intruder (including human trespassers) out of the area with their ears ringing.

Besides their guard and alarm calls, ospreys also swoop down upon, dive at and chase intruders that violate the osprey's territorial space. Male ospreys tend to engage in longer chases when in pursuit of enemies, while females usually restrict their chases to intruders close to the nest. Some ospreys are far more aggressive than others, and it is the unlucky intruder that assumes that the next nesting pair it approaches will be as easy to dupe as the last.

Although ospreys are generally non-combative, and are relatively taciturn as they go about the business of feeding and providing for their families, they will use their wings and talons in defense of their nest and young, although they rarely attack humans. Ospreys do their best to defend their territories, but some persistent birds and animals do succeed in stealing eggs and young in spite of the parents' best efforts.

Fights between ospreys occur most often over nest sites than over mates, and some ospreys have been injured and even killed as a result of such territorial conflicts, but such battles are considered extremely rare in any colony.

The begging call is uttered primarily by females toward their mates, which may or may not respond with food, attention, or both. Osprey females beg more often than they are fed, and researchers are not sure what it is that ultimately makes the male respond, or fail to respond, to the female's incessant begging. It may simply be that some males are quicker to respond than others. Nesting females will resort to hunting if no male responds, but not as enthusiastically as single or unmated females.

Back Home Again

When ospreys return to their natal nesting sites in spring from their wintering grounds, their arrival usually coincides with the appearance of their

Osprey nests are large, heavy structures that are refurbished each year by the mated pair.

primary food source. In New England, for example, it is the spring herring spawn that is the initial focus of returning ospreys. Some birds return to their nesting grounds weeks before the true thaw, actually pairing, breeding and laying eggs before winter's ice is fully gone. Fishing at such times is done in any available open water, particularly near rapids and dams. In general, such early breeding is done by pairs with established nests near exposed water, where fish can readily be taken. In some extreme northern parts of their range, ospreys will attempt to propagate early, but the young may not fledge in time to beat an early fall freeze-up.

The gradual northward warming trends of spring are closely followed by migrating ospreys, and breeding dates seem to follow latitudinal lines. For example, Delaware Bay ospreys nest and breed earlier than Connecticut birds, which may be a week or two ahead of Maine ospreys, and so on up into Canada and Labrador.

"Springtime" is a nebulous term in the north country, where ice-out may not occur until late April or early May. One cannot predict with certainty the precise date that the large inland lakes will open up, and local lotteries are held in some New England communities, with winnings going to the one who predicts, to the hour, when the lakes of Moosehead, Champlain or Winnepesaukee will be ice-free. It is not wise to bet on the spring arrival of ospreys, however. In New England, the season's first osprey arrivals are generally reported from late March to early April, and almost immediately afterward, the brood-rearing season begins.

Nesting

Male ospreys usually arrive at the nesting grounds first, generally a few days before the females. Harsh weather may delay pairing and nesting for some time, and extremely bad weather can drive birds away from their preferred coastal nesting sites to more sheltered inland areas, where they will sit, hunched forlornly on their perches, to ride out the storm.

Established pairs nearly always return to claim their previous-year's nest site, many times for a decade or more in succession, or until one partner is lost or the nest has been destroyed.

Osprey nests are located so that the birds can access them on the wing.

Following pages: Ospreys continue to use the same nest site for a decade or more.

Nesting preferences often restrict some hawk species, but the osprey is much easier to please than most. It will nest from high to low branches on trees, on manmade structures, and even on the ground. New pairs, or those birds that must find new sites, take longer to complete the breeding process, as it can take weeks for the birds to try out several trees in not-always-successful efforts to construct a new nest.

Ospreys are not picky about selecting new sites, but the sheer physics of creating a huge, heavy mass of sticks, limbs and other materials demands that a site be strong, sturdy and durable, a skill that can only come with time and experience.

It is the female osprey that decides which nest site will be used, and it is she that finally lays the eggs and cares directly for the young. Because good, isolated nest sites must include proximity to water and food, finding the right site is not as easy as it may seem. Preferred nest sites include tall trees, ideally flat-topped and free of overhangs and other obstacles, as ospreys have long, narrow wings not designed for quick boreal maneuvering. The ideal nest site should be easy to soar or glide into from the air. For this reason, cliffs and rocky bluffs are often utilized.

In North America, ospreys readily and enthusiastically utilize artificial nest platforms. In one study, over 65 percent of one osprey colony's breeding birds chose platforms over natural nest sites. Swamps and islands free of predators are the preferred nest location, and when platform sites are readily available in such habitat, the osprey's nesting success rate is extraordinarily high.

The list of manmade structures suitable for osprey nest sites seems almost endless, and is bound by nothing more than access to water and an abundant food supply nearby. Ospreys will readily nest on power poles, trestles, high voltage towers, channel markers and buoys, duck blinds, and just about any other elevated structure, regardless of its height over water.

Although ospreys will build nests over land, they show a marked preference for over-water sites, perhaps because only winged predators can find them there, significantly reducing the number of attackers the osprey family must deal with.

The osprey's awareness of predators, particularly land-based scavengers such as raccoons, foxes, minks, dogs, cats and weasels, is believed to influence their choice of islands as nesting sites. It is estimated that at least half of the world's osprey nests are built on such islands. In fact, most of the largest,

Ospreys readily utilize artificial structures for nesting as long as adequate food supplies exist nearby.

densest osprey colonies in the world are established on island sites. For example, in one colony on Great White Island in Mexico's San Ignacia Lagoon, over one hundred breeding pairs were reported along one three-mile strip, indicating that ospreys can thrive when shallow, productive waters are found near abundant nest sites. This is the largest known concentration of osprey nest sites in the world. In addition, ospreys readily build ground nests in such habitat. It is believed that the lack of land-based predators. makes the ospreys feel safer about building low-level nests.

Nests are heavily constructed of sticks, bones, fur, skins and all sorts of "trash" scavenged from land and water near the nest site. Nest repairs are made each year, and are easy to track due to the placement of fresh material on the top and in the cup of the nest. Ospreys will attempt to rebuild a damaged nest at least once, and sometimes twice, before abandoning the project.

Interestingly, house sparrows, grackles and other small birds often build their nests in osprey nests, apparently to make use of the protection provided by the larger birds.

Whether for social or antagonistic reasons, ospreys seem to prefer nesting close to other ospreys, often as close as about 160 feet apart. Some colonies have ospreys nesting as close as 60 feet apart, but the norm is about 4,000 feet. This may be that established pairs attract inexperienced birds, or that some birds see the opportunity to "steal" established nest sites.

Courtship and Breeding

It's not difficult for the astute observer to determine when the male osprey is courting. Like most other creatures, the osprey is conspicuous in his mating display, and, like most other birds, the osprey's amorous performances depend heavily on ritual flight patterns—which it may also use to reflect agitation of a different sort at other times of the year, such as when threatened or upset by creatures other than receptive female ospreys.

The male begins his courtship display with a high-pitched, continuous call uttered as he soars high overhead, legs dangling, often with a fish or some nesting material clutched in his talons (although he may also conduct his display flight without such props).

The flight display is a slow, roller coaster pattern, not at all similar to standard hunting or nest-building flights. It is obviously designed to attract the attention of the nearby female, and is most common among single males,

This uninterested female is rejecting the male's advances.

although some long-time mated males may perform the display as well, perhaps to strengthen the pair bond.

Osprey mating displays are generally performed in clear, fair weather, usually close to the chosen nest site. There are two standard display patterns exhibited by the male: an up-and-down, rolling pattern punctuated by a brief hover at the peak of each aerial "hill"; and a second pattern that is a hover continued for some time as the bird rises and falls at varying heights.

Although osprey courtship flights are perhaps the most dramatic and inspirational aspect of the osprey's spring courtship ritual, what really matters to a female when choosing a mate is not his clever aerial antics, but his ability to provide food to her and her brood. After all, osprey females receive almost all of their food from their mates prior to laying the eggs through fledging of the young; so the selection of a good provider is, for all practical purposes, a matter of life and death.

For females, selection of a mate begins when the female selects a nest site (or returns to an established nest) and begins her begging call. An established mate usually responds, or a new suitor will take over, but a female will feed herself if no male appears, though not as enthusiastically once egg laying commences.

The male osprey often strokes the female's back with his talons prior to breeding.

63

The osprey female begs for food from any nearby males, including her established mate, but she will also beg from nearby bachelors. Males bringing food select a perch away from the nest site, then pause to eat part of the fish (usually the head and tail sections) before delivering the remaining pieces to the female. Hungry females beg incessantly to all nearby males, but it is usually only the paired mate that offers her a meal.

Younger paired males are not always as generous as older, established males when it comes to feeding the females. The younger males often hide or protect their catch from the begging female in a posture known as "mantling," in which the male hunches over his catch with outstretched wings. Older, experienced males surrender a meal more willingly.

What is perhaps most interesting about the osprey pairing process is that well-fed females are less likely to beg food from or copulate with other males, indicating that the courtship feeding ritual may be one way that ospreys guarantee long-lasting mate relationships.

The male not only feeds his chosen mate, which keeps her close to the nest, but he also defends her and the nest site from other males. During the period when the female is most fertile, the male swoops low around the female whenever she leaves the nest, and often touches her lightly on the back or neck with closed talons if she strays too far or tarries too long.

Although feeding is important in pair bonding, it has been suggested by some researchers that the availability of a solid, secure nest site is the crucial factor in whether or not a female ultimately stays with a particular male. Osprey pairs rarely separate, but when they do, it is often because attempts at nesting failed. It is assumed by experts that the birds actually become more attached to the nest site than to each other, and that is what keeps most osprey pairs together over time. Still, while males do not ordinarily abandon a nest site unless the nest structure is destroyed or the nesting attempt is otherwise thwarted, it seems that females rarely leave a mate unless the male provides no food for her or the young.

Young ospreys tend to mate with birds their own age, but older birds, especially those into their second decade, tend to select younger mates, no doubt due to the fact that, in most populations, the majority of available single birds are usually three- to four-year-olds mating for the first time.

When ospreys select a nest site and begin serious courtship feeding, mating occurs at random, and not always at or near the nest. The male approaches the female from above, wings flapping, closed talons out-stretched, and rests precariously on the female's back. If the female is receptive, she tips forward, tail raised, allowing the male's tail to swivel tightly under hers until cloacal contact is made and the transfer of sperm is completed.

Unreceptive females maintain a horizontal position so that the male is unable to complete the act, and is left flapping foolishly in the wind until he slides off or gives up and moves away from the uninterested female.

A few ospreys indulge in polygyny, or mated trios, where one male breeds successfully with two females. This trait is most prevalent whenever male osprey mortality is especially high in a colony or population, and is observed in less than 2 percent of all nesting pairs.

The male in these cases treats both nesting females, nests and clutches as his own, breeding, feeding and defending them with equal care and attention, usually successfully, right through fledging of the young.

It is generally true that polygynous males establish nests that are close together, perhaps for convenience, as he will be doubly busy in his responsibilities as provider and defender for the nest.

Occasionally, two females will share a single nest with one male, but this is extremely rare, because female ospreys are generally intolerant of intruders or visitors to the nest. Studies in osprey polygyny are incomplete, but it has

Grass, twigs, and other materials are added to the nest throughout the nesting season.

been suggested that it may be mother/daughter or sister/sister pairings that facilitate the occurrence. It may also be a lack of sufficient food, mates or nesting sites that leads to these unusual circumstances.

Raising the Brood

Once mated, ospreys lay three and occasionally four eggs 10 to 39 days after arriving in their breeding territory. Nest building, mating and breeding take more time for younger, inexperienced birds than for older, established pairs, so there are cases where some ospreys will be weeks behind the main population at any point in the reproductive process.

Migratory ospreys (which includes most of the North American varieties) lay eggs in the spring, while resident birds, particularly those in Florida and South America, breed in winter, usually from December to February. Australasian ospreys, meanwhile, lay their eggs from May through August, which corresponds with that region's winter period.

Incubation by the female begins after the first egg is laid.

In most migratory populations, early layers predominate, and most of the population in a given area builds nests, breeds and mates at about the same time.

Osprey eggs are about the size of normal chicken eggs, and vary in color from white to light brown, splashed with varying shades of red, brown and gray blotches. Two to four eggs are laid one or two days apart, with later eggs being generally lighter and smaller than the first ones.

The eggs hatch in the same sequence as they were laid, which means that the younger chicks are usually smaller and weaker than their older siblings, and their survival rate is therefore much lower.

Both male and female ospreys participate in incubation, although females spend more time at it, especially through the night. Males that are not incubating don't necessarily spend their spare time hunting or feeding their mates, but they do spend a great deal of time perched at or near the nest, possibly guarding the females and eggs against intruders.

Incubation shifts can last a few minutes or for several hours, and the male usually, though not always, delivers a fish to the female when he takes his turn over the eggs.

Osprey eggs hatch an average of five to six weeks after laying. If the eggs are stolen, destroyed or become otherwise ruined during the first laying, a second clutch is often attempted, generally about three weeks after the first clutch fails.

Osprey chicks arrive weak, wet and helpless, entering the world about one or two days after they first begin pipping the shell. Down covers most of their body, and their eyes open within hours of hatching, at which point they begin taking food from the parents. The female accepts a fish from the male (which may already have eaten the head section) and, in many cases, she immediately eats the tail or anterior sections before she begins tearing off small bits of flesh from the body of the fish to present to the chicks.

The female keeps the nest clean during the nesting season by removing food, regurgitated indigestibles, feces and other debris. The nest is constantly renovated during the nesting period to cover or discard uneaten fish and other leftovers.

The young ospreys quickly develop a second coating of light down, usually about ten days after hatching, and the crop soon bulges with food, an adaptation that allows osprey parents more free time between feedings than most other birds.

Chick Development

For the next two weeks, osprey chicks enter what is referred to by biologists as their "reptilian stage," in which they are black, scaly-looking and aggressive toward each other. Changes in coloration now become apparent. A light tan streak runs down the chicks' backs, and their feet become bluish gray with long, black claws.

Feathers start replacing down at about two weeks of age, when pin feathers begin to appear on the head and neck of the chicks. Darker body feathers follow, with primaries, secondaries and wing and tail feathers developing at about three weeks of age.

Within thirty days of hatching, young ospreys have increased in size to about 75 percent of their adult body weight. To achieve this rate of growth, the male osprey (one with a single mate and three chicks) must hunt for three to four hours daily. However, males usually spend less than 35 percent of their day foraging, and this may have some impact on chick survival. Researchers have not discovered why male ospreys are so "lazy," but it may be more a question of ensuring the survival of the adult breeders than any lack of ambition on the male's part.

Small broods demand less food than do large broods, and there is a significant loss of weight in adults, especially females, when too many chicks are begging for food. Competition among chicks, and caution on the part of osprey parents, are major reasons why ospreys don't raise larger broods in the manner of ducks or chickens.

Osprey chicks are voracious eaters and grow quickly when adequate food is available.

Osprey chicks leave the nest about sixty-three days after hatching. Perhaps not surprisingly, migratory ospreys seem to mature faster than non-migratory birds. This may be due to the fact that migratory ospreys must hasten the fledging process in anticipation of moving south at the end of the nesting season, or it may simply be that year-round resident birds are not as well nourished as their long-distance relatives, which time their breeding period to the peak abundance of their prey species.

Life in the Nest

Lest one think that all is joy and harmony in an osprey nest, researchers have found that the availability of food often determines the survival of the young. Deaths occur, not necessarily by starvation, but due to competition for what food is available. A dominant chick, for example, being the oldest and largest of the brood, may attack or even eject smaller siblings from the

The male osprey spends nearly all its daylight hours fishing during the nesting season.

nest in order to keep most of the food for itself. Such fights invariably occur when food is scarce but such instances have been recorded when fish was delivered frequently and in plenty by the parents.

Osprey parents do not interfere in such sibling rivalries, not even to intervene when a chick is on the verge of being tossed from the nest by an older nestmate. It is apparent from all this that less food means fewer survivors, and if only one of four osprey chicks survive to fledge, it is probably best for the population, rather than having several weakened chicks fighting over a reduced or dwindling food supply.

In spite of endless hours of study, osprey researchers still cannot begin to guess how much fish a young nestling eats per meal or per day, nor even how much food it takes to nourish a chick to maturity. While feeding nestlings, it has been noted that the male osprey rarely gives up his portion of each fish he presents to the nest, but the female often does. It may be that the effort expended by the male in finding, catching and transporting his catch to the nest requires a higher caloric intake, or it may simply be that the female is bound by the code of motherhood to see that her chicks are fed first.

Fly, Fly Away!

Just prior to fledging, food is brought less frequently by the male, perhaps as a way to encourage the chicks to depart and begin hunting on their own. Now eight weeks old, about two weeks before fledging takes place, the young practice their wingbeats within the nest, with lots of flapping, jumping and flopping about in awkward caricature of the graceful, expert flyers they will soon become.

Many young ospreys leave the nest more by default than by design. A gust of wind, a bump from another chick, or simply the force of all that energetic practice suddenly lifts the fledgling from the nest. Invariably, if not somewhat awkwardly, the young ospreys manage to spread their wings and soar out over the water to the safety of the nearest perch.

As if making fledging a community event within the colony, young ospreys often flap and flutter toward other nests, switching places with their young colony mates, sometimes several times in the process of learning to fly. Like youngsters everywhere, it's the younger, put-upon chicks that seem to switch nests most often, and they, in turn, seek nests where they can be the dominant ones for a change.

Following pages: These young ospreys are almost ready to fledge.

While osprey parents often encourage fledglings to fly and hunt, it has been shown that orphaned or hacked osprey fledglings will actively hunt for food on their own, with no preliminary training at all. Some osprey parents do teach their young to hunt by dropping fish in midair for them to catch. Usually missing the prize at first, the young ospreys quickly learn to catch the fish in the air, and from this they gradually learn to take fish from the water.

As older osprey chicks fledge, the younger birds in a nest will continue to be cared for by the parents until all are gone. Even during fledging, the female osprey does not take part in finding food for the young, but allows the male to continue providing fresh fish for the nest.

The young ospreys may linger in the vicinity of the nest or colony through late summer, but, by September, the nests of migratory osprey colonies are empty and quiet, and the birds are gone for the season, not to return until the following spring.

Osprey Survival

Survival of fledged ospreys to breeding age is usually less than 50 percent, but it has been shown that the best osprey parents usually produce the most long-term survivors, and this holds true from colony to colony, worldwide. Also, experienced males are apparently more critical than experienced females when it comes to successfully fledging young, as even experienced females may fail to raise a brood when paired with an inexperienced male provider. Still, an estimated 85 percent of adult ospreys survive to the next year, and most ospreys live to between ten and thirteen years of age in the wild.

Older ospreys do seem to produce the most young, but the apparent cost of nesting success causes a higher mortality rate for older, experienced birds. According to Poole, some 30 percent of osprey young will be alive one year after fledging; 17 percent after eight years; and only six to eight adults will be alive at twelve years of age. It is encouraging to note that at least three cases have been documented where ospreys over twenty-four years old had returned to their natal breeding areas, a record for the species, and an astounding accomplishment for any wild bird, given the barriers to survival that exist in nature.

Young ospreys may linger near the nest through late summer.

Following pages: Tending and maintaining the nest is a continuous, full-time job for the male.

Chapter
Four

At Home and Away

The estimated U.S. population of nesting ospreys was determined most recently by researcher Larry Houghton (in 1994) at about 14,000 nesting pairs, although many biologists will admit that modern population inventory techniques may yet lag behind the osprey's ability to establish new territories. While researchers are often forced, by budgetary or staffing limits, to make their annual nest-site counts within strict watershed or coastal marshland boundaries, the osprey is under no such restrictions. It is not uncommon to find established, long-term nest sites on some very small, scientifically insignificant (and often overlooked) inland bogs, ponds and flowages. In one Maine study, for example, a 49 percent increase in survey flight time resulted in a 330 percent increase in osprey nest sightings! Flight time in this case was only 46 hours, so it seems certain that ospreys find suitable nest sites and plenty of food in some relatively small areas, often well away from traditional, major watersheds, bays and estuaries, where they gradually establish new colonies in which to raise their young.

Most ospreys live to be 10 to 13 years old in the wild.

In fact, according to Maine biologist Alan Hutchinson, who is presently in charge of that state's endangered and non-game research program, a 1980s study of osprey nest sites was abandoned when it became obvious that there were many more ospreys nesting in the state than researchers could adequately and accurately count. "We gave up when we estimated about 2,000 nesting pairs, but we are sure that there are many more ospreys than that in Maine," Hutchinson said.

Researchers estimate that 60 to 80 percent of the active osprey nests in the United States have been located at least once in the last thirty years. But it also has been pointed out that ospreys do not need to establish or defend distinct home territories, because food is usually so abundant in their preferred estuarine habitat there is plenty to go around. In addition, fish routinely move from place to place along coastlines and river systems, so the equally mobile osprey is able to hunt successfully wherever it chooses.

It is a tribute to the adaptability of the osprey that the species has been able, with some help from humans, to disprove 1970-era "silent spring" predictions of "extinction within twenty years." Ospreys can live for two decades or more in the wild, and have learned to adapt to radical habitat changes that would, and some-times do, cause some species to abandon nest sites and seek other territories.

Ospreys will nest wherever food supplies are abundant.

For example, active osprey nests can be found on Pennsylvania's Susquehanna River within sight of the busy Harrisburg airport, literally in the shadow of nearby Three Mile Island. Fishermen, duck hunters and recreational boaters share the river with hovering ospreys all summer, and the birds continue to conduct their business, seemingly oblivious to the equally industrious humans below—proving that wherever they are found around the world, ospreys can, and do, prosper in areas where other, less tolerant raptors have been driven out.

Most abundant on sea coasts and somewhat less numerous inland, ospreys in North America range near water along the Atlantic Coast, including Chesapeake Bay, and into the Great Lakes region. They are fairly common on lakes, rivers and ponds in the northern boreal forest from Newfoundland west to the Pacific Coast. Ospreys are less common in parts of Montana, Idaho, Wyoming and elsewhere in the central United States, but, especially during fall and spring migrations, are likely to linger anywhere in this region while en route to traditional nesting or wintering grounds.

The U.S. population is heaviest along the East Coast. About 50 percent of all U.S. ospreys nest within foraging distance of the Atlantic seaboard and the Gulf of Mexico. In this area, Chesapeake Bay and adjoining watersheds support an estimated 2,000 breeding pairs, or some 20 percent of the U.S. total. Florida holds another 20 percent, as does Maine. A second, smaller, somewhat isolated U.S. population exists in northern Michigan, Wisconsin and Minnesota. These birds tend to nest inland on lakes, ponds and rivers. An estimated 650 breeding pairs are thought to exist in this region; they are considered to be Canadian birds because the northern population expanded into the region following the decimation of the U.S. colony in the 1960s.

A scattering of ospreys exists in Alaska and Canada in coniferous forests, nesting along inland lakes and rivers, but this is considered to be the extreme northern limit for these birds, as the nesting season is often too short to allow timely fledging of young.

Western ospreys are most common near artificial reservoirs (the only water available in many areas). Few ospreys are found near the Pacific Coast, most likely because the shoreline habitat is too steep for nesting, and the water too deep for foraging.

Ospreys nesting and breeding in the United States traditionally winter in the Caribbean, Central America and northern South America, except for a

Wintering ospreys spend most of their time resting and preening.

few birds that remain along the Gulf Coast, southern California and southern Florida, where ospreys are year-round residents.

Ospreys are now common in areas not normally depicted on standard osprey range maps. In addition to the North American population, ospreys can be found in upper South America, Africa, Asia and coastal Australia, and breed in North America, Eurasia, Africa and Australia.

Ospreys do not yet breed in South America or Indo Malaysia (India and Southeast Asia), an oddity of behavior that researchers continue to investigate. In essence, the osprey either breeds or migrates on all major continents except South America, where it does winter; and except Antarctica, where the climate is simply too harsh to support any bird whose primary diet consists of live, surface-caught fish. It appears that Australian ospreys are non-migratory, although there has been little intense study of this population. Also, the *ridgwayi* (Caribbean) subspecies is also thought to be non-migratory.

Fall Migration

For most U.S. osprey populations, the frenzy of the nesting season winds down in late August and September. The young leave the nest to hunt on their own and, one by one, the gradual dispersal of ospreys to their tradition-al wintering grounds begins. By mid-October, most northeastern U.S. osprey colonies are empty, and adults and newly-fledged juveniles begin to drift their way south and east.

In general, all ospreys of a region follow the same flight paths to their wintering grounds, but some migration studies have shown higher rates of either adult or juvenile birds, suggesting that younger ospreys may follow different flight paths than their parents in reaching their post-fledging homes. It appears that northeastern U.S. ospreys follow that region's major mountain ranges and ridge lines in their southward travels. Some northeastern ospreys have been known to wander nearly to the Mississippi River as they meander south, but the majority of these banded birds seem to closely follow the Atlantic coastline. Researchers believe that this may be due to the fact that most ospreys are hatched and fledged in coastal colonies, so it would be rea-sonable for them to utilize the familiar salt coast in their southward naviga-tion. Ospreys do not build huge reserves of fat prior to migrating, so it may be that coastal routes simply ensure more food supplies en route.

Some ospreys utilize riverine habitat in the fall, suggesting that these birds follow inland watercourses to find their winter haunts. Most other birds of prey avoid lengthy water crossings due to a lack of updrafts and thermal currents, which are so crucial to soaring, but ospreys have no such problem. Migrating ospreys are often seen on islands far out to sea in the Caribbean and the Mediterranean, and ospreys have been observed flying strongly as much as 125 miles off shore, exhibiting no desire to land or rest on flotsam or passing ships.

Ospreys also cross wide expanses of land while migrating, including, in at least one documented case, the entire 1,290 miles of North Africa's Sahara Desert, a trip that would take two days or more at the relatively high rate of 18 to 30 mph. Ospreys do fly strong and hard while migrating, however. At Hawk Mountain, Pennsylvania, one osprey was clocked, soaring, at 80 mph!

Ospreys often travel over long water distances at night, apparently preferring to fly overland routes during the daylight hours. In a lifetime of fifteen years, an osprey may travel in excess of 62,000 miles to and from its nest sites and wintering grounds.

Coastal estuaries provide ideal habitat for wintering ospreys.

U.S. ospreys tend to migrate along routes compatible with their breeding region. For example, western U.S. ospreys winter along the Gulf Coast of Mexico, rarely crossing the Mississippi en route. Great Lakes populations winter in the western Gulf region of Florida, generally keeping between the Mississippi and the eastern inland mountains while traveling. East coastal birds winter along the East Coast of Florida, the Caribbean, and on the northern coast of South America.

The U.S. osprey migration may begin as early as late August, continuing through the latter part of November and early December. The majority of ospreys arrive at their wintering grounds in October. The relatively long period of osprey migration is influenced by the fact that some ospreys breed and fledge their young longer than others, and not all ospreys travel south at the same rate. In addition, juvenile ospreys seem to be among the last to join the species' southward exodus. It appears that while all ospreys leave their breeding grounds at the same time, they don't all travel at the same pace. In general, northern birds travel more slowly than their southern counterparts, and southern colonies tend to complete their migration sooner.

All ospreys migrate alone, including juveniles. Researchers have found that juvenile ospreys often complete their southward journeys as quickly and efficiently as adults, which suggests that navigational skills may be inherited instincts, and that imprinting of landmarks, or learning by experience, is not the case, at least in ospreys.

Winter migration continues at a reduced pace through November, and evidence of gradual northward movement (in northeastern U.S. colonies) has been documented as early as March. Winter, for ospreys, seems to be that period generally between December and late February.

While most U.S. ospreys head south to the tropics in winter, some remain inland during the winter. These birds are likely to be sick, injured or otherwise unable to make the trip south.

Wintering Range

Just as ospreys are loyal to their natal nesting and foraging sites, they also seem partial to familiar wintering areas, and most will return to the same winter colonies each year.

Once back on their winter range, ospreys spend their time feeding, resting and loafing, primarily along coastal bays and estuaries; particularly on shallow, open tidal flats and river mouths—places where surface-dwelling fish are abundant. In one study, it was estimated that, in one West African river

Ospreys generally return to traditional wintering areas each year.

delta alone, some 30,000 tons of fish were eaten each winter by ospreys and other fish-eating birds.

Ospreys on their wintering grounds are remarkably gregarious for birds that, same species or not, are competing for the same prey. One researcher counted twenty-five ospreys perched within 330 feet, and spotted five ospreys perched on a log only 16 feet long. While a lack of suitable feeding and perching sites may cause such "stacking" of birds, actively hunting ospreys were also seen to travel in flocks as well. In fact, like gulls, ospreys hovering and diving often stimulated other ospreys to join in on the feast.

Following pages: Ospreys begin their spring migration as early as March.

In some wintering areas, a lack of suitable perch sites does create a degree of competition between colonized birds, but the osprey's ability to fly, coupled with its innate ability to adapt to most any otherwise limiting situation, invariably results in a smooth, orderly dispersal of birds.

Ospreys may spend the winter along the coast, or they may move inland to seek suitable off-season quarters. Avoidance of predators, including raccoons, alligators and snakes, always a consideration to ospreys no matter where they are found, has some bearing on the choices they make when dispersing within their winter range.

Spring Migration

Ospreys begin leaving their wintering grounds in early March, gradually moving north again in an apparently planned "shuffle" designed to place them on their nesting sites as early in spring as possible. Northern-nesting birds leave earliest in order to arrive at their nest sites on time for efficient breeding and fledging of young.

Spring migration takes place at a much faster pace than does the osprey's leisurely southward movement, as if the urgency of the season somehow hastens them northward. The spring exodus takes about one-third the time, as if the birds know that the earliest nesters produce the most surviving young.

Yearling ospreys remain on the wintering grounds for another eighteen months or more, until they make their first return trip to their natal nest sites, at around age two.

Two-year-old, non-breeding ospreys leave later and travel at a much slower pace than breeding adults, further suggesting that the urgency of the season is the reason adult birds leave earlier and travel fastest.

According to biologist Larry Rymon, two-year-old ospreys return to their natal nest sites as late as June, which is too late for them to be involved in breeding. It is not known if these birds are even physiologically capable of breeding. It appears that these non-breeding "adolescent" ospreys just dally around their former parents' nest sites, in some cases actually trying to take over the site, apparently in preparation for their own breeding activities, which will take place the following year. For several weeks, these "teenage" ospreys actually become a nuisance to the nesting female, and can even cause nest abandonment if they are especially persistent and can't be easily driven off.

Any tall, solid structure, natural or artificial, will satisfy the nesting needs of breeding ospreys.

In their spare time, these pre-adult birds spend most of their days exploring, seeking nest sites of their own, and may even build nests if an existing site isn't available.

While they do not help other breeding birds in any way, they have been known to "fill in" for or replace one breeding partner of the same sex when that partner is killed or fails to perform its duties.

Taken by the Wind

The question of why ospreys even bother to migrate at all, since they can withstand winter cold, is answered by the fact that their prey are simply unavailable to them in numbers large enough to sustain them over winter. In cold weather, cold-blooded fish seek deeper water, and so even when open-water conditions prevail in winter, there are not enough fish available within the osprey's critical three-foot depth of operation.

While scientists believe that it is the osprey's "internal clock" which dictates when migration will begin, it is interesting to note that ospreys begin arriving on their nesting grounds within days of ice-out. How they know or sense the event is still a matter of curiosity among researchers. Conversely, ospreys leave their nesting grounds on their southward journeys well before food becomes scarce or unavailable, so it is believed that something other than hunger is the driving force behind the osprey's seasonal movements.

So-called resident birds, those ospreys which remain in subtropical latitudes for

Competition for mates begins as soon as ospreys arrive at their spring nesting sites.

most of their lives, do move somewhat, although usually less than sixty miles within their home range. In these populations, adult birds remain close to their nesting sites, perhaps because such sites are difficult to acquire and because much time is invested in building and maintaining them. In most cases, it is young, non-breeding birds that disperse, albeit locally, from their natal nest sites.

By mid-March, most migratory osprey wintering sites are barren of all but yearling birds, and the endless cycle of osprey life and living begins again.

Predator-proof nest sites are critical to osprey nesting success.

Following pages: Young osprey testing its wings for flight.

Chapter
Five

Threats to Osprey Survival

I n an ideal world, ospreys would have unlimited, unmolested nest sites
with plenty of food, endless fair weather, and no predators to contend
with. Human intrusion would be minimal, and there would be no
related threats involving chemical contamination, pollution, nesting
conflicts or poaching of eggs, nests or young.

Of course, the perfect world does not exist for any of us, but a working
knowledge of what benefits an osprey family, and what doesn't, will go far in
ensuring that future disasters, large and small, are kept to a minimum.

Like all other wild animals, ospreys are ever at the mercy of the elements,
predators (including humans), accidents and misfortunes. Banded migratory
ospreys are often recovered only after injury, drowning, exhaustion or death
has taken them, suggesting that a great many ospreys succumb, not to old
age, but to the everyday hazards of raptorial life.

Unmated and adolescent ospreys return to their natal colonies in spring,
but may not nest or breed until the following year.

Predation

It is rare for anyone to see an osprey becoming a victim of a predator, and this includes researchers who, by the nature of their work, spend more time observing and living with ospreys than anyone else. Still, predation definitely does occur, most commonly at night during the nesting period. Eggs and young are the primary victims of nocturnal marauders, but some adults, primarily incubating females, may be taken from the nest after dark, invariably by owls.

Though adult ospreys do defend their nests with vigor, a determined raccoon, fox, skunk or similar land-based predator (domestic dogs and cats also enter the mix as infrequent opportunists), will raid any nest they can reach in spite of the sharp talons and beating wings of an enraged osprey parent.

The best way to negate such predation is for ospreys to build all of their nests out of the reach of such predators, ideally on islands (which most land-based predators can't reach) or on tall, slippery poles, such as those provided by humans. Some people put sheet-metal anti-predator guards around the bases of the tree or pole to deter predators from climbing into the nests.

Although predation occurs, natural enemies to the osprey are few.

Following pages: Volunteers are helping ospreys by constructing boxes, platforms, poles and other artificial nesting structures.

In the 1990s, predation of ospreys may well increase as numbers of raccoons, foxes, mink and skunks continue to skyrocket, especially in the Northeast, due primarily to a slump in the fur garment industry and associated declines in fur trapping.

Avian Competition

Competition between ospreys and other birds of prey does exist, however infrequently. African fish eagles, for example, are occasionally aggressive toward ospreys, as are other, similar fish-eaters around the world. But, in situations where such antagonistic behavior is common, the osprey will often resort to fish-stealing antics of its own in an attempt to even the score.

In the avian pecking order, it is apparent that bigger is dominant, even between species. For example, a bird larger than an osprey such as a bald eagle, will put forth a serious, often successful, effort to steal an osprey's catch, while a larger osprey will return the favor by attempting to intimidate a fresh-caught fish from some lesser adversary. Events of this sort are usually spur of the moment, opportunistic efforts, however, and border on the level of bullying.

There have been no documented cases of an osprey dying or being driven out of a territory as a result of having its meals stolen by the occasional thief. Because ospreys are among the most successful of avian anglers, it may be that other species recognize the osprey's prodigious fishing skills, and simply use intimidation as a way to garner the occasional free meal.

In any event, the osprey recovers quickly from such losses, and soon captures another fish for its own use, in spite of the obnoxious interloper.

Human Interference

Prior to the 1970s, hunting was considered a viable threat to osprey populations both inside and outside the United States, but in the decades since, an enlightened public has apparently turned to other forms of entertainment and income, because shooting deaths of ospreys are not now considered an exceptional problem (a threat to the species' survival in the U.S.). Minor hotspots do exist in other parts of the world, however, primarily in true wilderness areas, where primitive tribes still depend on wildlife for survival. For example, most northern European ospreys migrate to tropical

Ospreys will aggressively defend their territories against interlopers.

New laws and wildlife programs ensure the success of breeding populations.

areas in winter, and some of these birds are shot by subsistence hunters along the way. In fact, substantial numbers of Scottish-bred ospreys, all banded for recovery, were killed in this way.

Europeans, particularly, continue to be a threat to ospreys in this regard. Historically, poaching of ospreys, their young and eggs by market hunters had decimated osprey populations in many areas of Britain and Scotland prior to 1960, and the birds were declared extinct in Britain as early as 1910. Although laws protecting raptors in the United States were passed in the early 1970s, it wasn't until 1996 that the European Parliament voted to close the European Union hunting season on seventy-four species of migrating birds (including various species of hawks, owls, kites, vultures, harriers, falcons and other raptors). Interestingly, the measure was passed by just nine votes, with France dissenting strongly on the grounds that the right to hunt migratory birds was "won through revolution" and is "an integral part of

French culture." Not all of the voting countries in the European Union agreed on specific dates for hunting of migratory bird species, and so many birds will still have to run the gauntlet of hunters in the region each spring and fall.

Subsistence shooting in parts of Central and South America continues to this day, and in the United States, ospreys are occasionally shot while in the act of taking fish from hatcheries or other waters where there is a perceived competition from popular, harvestable or marketable fish populations, although these events are considered rare.

In the United States and elsewhere in North America, laws protect birds of prey and exempt them from hunting. These laws and education programs aimed at examining and explaining the role and benefits of such birds, coupled with the elimination, through international treaties, of markets for bird feathers and parts, have reduced shootings of ospreys to the kind of random, thoughtless, spur-of-the-moment acts that will, in all likelihood, never be stopped. But, with strict enforcement of existing laws protecting ospreys and other birds of prey in the United States, illegal shootings of birds of prey—ospreys in particular—has diminished dramatically, and vandalism to nests and eggs has all but ended in most of the osprey's North American range.

The value of such protection is obvious, given that the loss of even one osprey can seriously impact a local breeding population. When one partner of an osprey pair is killed, the mate is likely to abandon the nest and may not breed again for several seasons. Many breeding-age ospreys may not pair up immediately after the loss of a partner, but they may return to their natal nest site without reproducing. For this reason, removal of even one breeding adult may have a serious impact on the long-term survival of a local population of ospreys.

Despite laws and continuing education programs detailing the value of raptors in the environment, a strong prejudice against birds of prey still exists in parts of the United States. Even today, many Southern quail plantations still enforce the unwritten policy that all hawks and owls seen near game-farm hunting fields are to be shot on sight. It is understood that the practice is illegal, but when pen-raised quail are valued at twelve dollars or more, and pheasants may cost twenty dollars each to produce, there is a perceived competition for these valuable birds, and so raptors are considered vermin by plantation owners.

Following pages: Ospreys are not adverse to building nests on utility poles.

In some countries, primitive tribes still hunt ospreys for meat, feathers, eggs and young, but studies have shown that most of the victims are young of the year, or surplus members of the population, and so the colony is not irreparably harmed by such subsistence hunting, except in those isolated cases where extended hunting in nesting areas continues unchecked by any sort of consideration for the future of the resource.

The influence of humans on osprey populations is undeniable. In some species, conflicts over human goals invariably end with *Homo sapiens* coming out the winner, regardless of the price to the vanquished wild species. In fact, it is a rare occurrence when humans do something for their own benefit that also favors wildlife, but, generally speaking, and aside from the effects of chemical contamination, human activity alone is not a threat to ospreys. In fact, some osprey colonies are enhanced when the efforts of humans include the construction of electrical towers, power poles, piers, buoys and similar over-water structures. It is when humans disturb the pairing, nesting or breeding process that ospreys react in a negative way. Although ospreys do tolerate human intrusion quite well, in fact better than most other raptors, there are times when an osprey is less tolerant of nosy, noisy or otherwise bothersome two-legged interlopers. In fact, it has been shown that some remote-nesting ospreys are much less tolerant of humans than birds that have become used to regular human activity. Because it is impossible to predict how long an osprey parent can be away from its nest before harm comes to the eggs or chicks, it is important that observers respect the osprey's "personal space." Repeated, prolonged close-quarter intrusions could cause the male or female osprey to leave the nest for an extended period, which, in stormy or cold weather, could result in the loss of eggs or the death by exposure of hatchlings.

Habitat Destruction

As with all Earth's creatures, habitat destruction is the greatest threat ospreys face as we enter a new century. As humans multiply, so does our need for sustenance, and the related losses to wildlife species, including ospreys, could be catastrophic in parts of the world. Coastal logging could eliminate whole nesting colonies of ospreys, and timber cutting along critical inland watersheds and lakes could devastate many of the colonies that have only recently begun to recover from the near-terminal effects of chemical contamination experienced in the mid-1900s.

Changes in watercourse flows, through damming and channelization projects, particularly in the South, has caused ospreys to abandon some traditional nesting grounds. In other areas, pollution and unchecked erosion have caused corresponding changes in fish habitat, to the point that adequate food stocks have been eliminated in former osprey breeding grounds.

Perhaps the greatest concern to osprey biologists is the continued clearing of tropical forests, especially those in traditional osprey wintering areas. The trickle-down effect of such rapid, radical changes in osprey habitats includes abandonment of nest sites, loss of fishing grounds due to excess siltation, erosion and surface temperature warming, all of which occur when long-standing forests are eliminated. This may cause local osprey populations to seek other forage sites, including hatchery ponds and other aquacultural operations, resulting in an increase in osprey shootings. In addition, when

This relatively elaborate artificial nest site features a useful, built-in perch for resting and feeding.

nesting sites become scarce in the osprey's natal colony, the birds may delay breeding until age five or six, nearly double the normal first-year breeding age of three or four years.

Also, the osprey's affinity for localized nesting sties can be its downfall, as was demonstrated by the near disaster caused by DDT/DDE contamination in the 1950s and 1960s, when affected osprey eggshells became so thin and brittle that the weight of the incubating parent collapsed them. Repeat nesting attempts also failed, and so although the osprey parents themselves were not always directly affected by chemical poisoning, destruction of the eggs could, in time, just as easily have eliminated whole colonies of ospreys. Because ospreys are extremely loyal to their natal nest sites, colonization of new areas is a slow process. If the ospreys won't move, and the chemical contamination is allowed to continue, it is easy to predict how the scenario will end.

Nest site intrusion, especially when coupled with extreme habitat destruction, can disrupt the osprey breeding process for many years. Armed with this knowledge, researchers and biologists can predict with relative certainty the effects of proposed habitat "improvement" projects on local osprey colonies.

Other Limiting Factors

Little research has been done on the mortality rates of yearling ospreys. They do not become attached to nest sites until their third or fourth years, and they are usually dispersed widely over their wintering grounds, so it is difficult to monitor their movements and habits. Still, researchers have suggested that at least 50 percent, if not more, of all osprey fledglings survive their first year, a phenomenal rate among birds in general, and among the highest rates for large raptors as well.

Like most other large predatory birds (and animals, for that matter), ospreys produce relatively few young. Researchers suspect that one major limiting factor is food, or the lack of it. Starvation is the number one killer of young ospreys, which is not always a reflection of the amount of food present, but of the limited availability of food created when a dominant (first-born) chick begins hoarding food and driving subordinate chicks from meals delivered by the male parent. While survival of the fittest may be an easy way to answer the question of why one chick survives and all others in

Larger nests such as this indicate that ospreys have used the site for several years.

the nest may perish, it's more accurate to say "survival of the first," because, among ospreys, it's the first-born chick that gets the first food, and is therefore the largest and most aggressive of the clutch.

There is room for discussion on this business of fitness, however, because when subordinate chicks are orphaned or abandoned and then placed in other nests, or are fed artificially by biologists, many of these "unfit" chicks survive to fledge and thrive as adults.

Starvation and reduced brood production is common in subtropical regions, which many observers find curious, because one would think that a warmer climate would mean food aplenty year-round. In truth, however, it is the seasonal "boom and bust" of the northern migratory forage species (including herring and menhaden) in the osprey food chain that is simply not found in subtropical regions. In most cases, the odds for chick survival increases with the abundance of food. When fish are plentiful, there is less fighting and competition among chicks, and survival rates are much higher as a result.

Late-nesters and repeat attempts at breeding have much lower success rates than ospreys which breed and nest successfully earlier in the season. It is generally young or newly mated pairs that fail to fledge their young,

Ospreys dine on a wide variety of fish.

First-born osprey chicks are most likely to survive to adulthood.

and simple inexperience that may be to blame in some cases. However, some studies have shown that entire colonies may fledge young at lower rates when breeding is delayed due to harsh weather, suggesting that age or experience might not be all of the equation in rooting out the cause of nesting failures in ospreys.

Ospreys have learned, through thousands of years of evolution, that more food does not necessarily translate into more chicks or better chick survival, a phenomenon researchers have only lately come to understand. For the good of the population, it is the fate of third or fourth chicks to be doomed to die prior to fledging, especially in areas where food is less abundant, but also where frequent, violent storms are common during the spring and early summer.

Humans have not yet found a way to manage marine fish species to the satisfaction of all, and the weather is just another important but uncontrollable limiting factor that ospreys are dependent upon. Prolonged stormy weather may make it difficult or impossible for the male osprey to hunt, and if such conditions continue unabated for prolonged periods, chicks may starve to death. Also, incubating females may abandon a clutch of eggs when severe weather threatens the nest, and abandoned young can become chilled or starve to death as a result.

Fortunately, chemical contamination and habitat loss can be monitored and managed, and when these are held in check, losses due to forage depletion and harsh weather can be absorbed into the population without severely affecting the population or colony as a whole.

Following pages: As long as healthy fish populations are available, ospreys will continue to thrive.

Chapter
Six

Ospreys and You

"**M**y goal is to have ospreys nesting in every available niche." With that lofty goal in mind, osprey expert Larry Rymon of East Stroudsburg University, who is credited with the first successful osprey hacking experiment in the United States, has issued a challenge, not only to himself, but to everyone who enjoys seeing and observing "fish hawks" in action. Some states now have areas that are devoid of ospreys that contain suitable habitat for them, and Rymon believes that osprey populations could be established in these places if hacking programs were instituted and if environmental contamination, habitat degradation and other threats could be reduced or eliminated.

What You Can Do

Like most other wildlife species, ospreys will respond to positive, favorable changes in their habitat. Perhaps the most common avenue amateur osprey fanciers can utilize is the installation of artificial nest sites. This has been a common practice in the United States since the 1700s, when colonial farmers

Ospreys often spread their wings to dry their feathers after a successful plunge.

put wagon wheels on posts near their barn yards to attract ospreys, which, the colonists hoped, would repel hawks and other unwanted predators.

Artificial nest sites may be live, topped-off trees with platforms attached, or any combination of poles, tripods and the like. Ospreys readily utilize such manmade sites, and have been known to actually wait impatiently nearby for human workers to finish installing platforms so the birds could begin nest building.

As long as such platforms are installed near water and are inaccessible by intruders (human and otherwise), they will nearly always be utilized, often for many years, by osprey colonies.

Platforms not only provide new nesting sites for first-year breeding ospreys, but they also serve as safe alternatives to the high-tension towers and electrical poles the birds often use, frequently at considerable risk to adults and young.

In many cases, humans who know of or construct backyard osprey nests guard them with a passion. These folks are probably the best neighbors the ospreys could hope for, as predation in such cases is kept to a minimum by the osprey's human benefactor. The ospreys reward that kindness by returning, year after year, to the same nests, entertaining their hosts with high-flying aerial displays, expert fishing demonstrations, and with luck and determination, the successful fledging of brand new ospreys.

Attractive as the idea of supplying artificial nest sites for ospreys may seem on the surface, keep in mind that such structures need annual maintenance to ensure that the nest will be there when the birds return to breed in following seasons.

Adult ospreys have been known to live over 20 years in the wild.

Following pages: Habitat preservation and pollution controls should keep ospreys soaring for generations to come.

The birds must also be protected from marauding predators of all types. If a platform is erected without considering the long-term objective of the platform plan, all of the effort involved may be wasted. Remember, osprey nest sites are often at a premium in some colonies, and when a site is destroyed, paired birds may fail to breed that season, and birds that lose their nest may not breed for several years following the event. For this reason, it is imperative that anyone wishing to construct an osprey nest consult with state endangered or non-game management experts before undertaking any nest site or habitat enhancement projects.

The Fiscal Alternative

In most states, the successful completion of important non-game management programs depends more on adequate funding than on initiative. Fortunately, nearly every state has an endangered or non-game species management program, and most are funded by annual income tax check-offs, general fund revenues, and/or private donations. Funding for such programs is critical to ospreys and other wildlife, because there is rarely room in any state's wildlife management program to include special treatment for non-funded wildlife projects.

Except during the breeding and nesting season, ospreys are solitary birds within the colony.

Following pages: Ospreys are tolerant of most other birds within their range unlike other, more territorial raptors.

Because osprey survival is ultimately in the hands of those who control and manipulate the environment, and because not all admirers of ospreys are able to get personally involved in habitat acquisition, nest-site construction, fisheries management or hacking programs, the only viable option is to support, with dollars, management and education programs designed to benefit these birds.

For those who are able, volunteering for endangered or non-game management project work is a possibility. Call your state wildlife management division and ask about volunteering for nest-site construction projects, habitat rejuvenation programs, or hacking experiments; or ask where to send funds to keep existing programs solvent and certain of a future.

Enjoying Ospreys the Right Way

To get the most out of osprey observation and study without frightening the birds or causing them to abandon nests or young, it is important to know how to approach and observe them properly.

When venturing into an osprey colony to observe or photograph nesting or feeding birds, it is important that you exercise great caution so that neither the parents or the nestlings are disturbed. Wear drab clothing and move slowly (without talking) into and out of the area. Travel alone rather

It is best to observe ospreys from a distance, using binoculars or a spotting scope to avoid disturbing them.

than with a distracting group. Observe nests and birds from a distance, and be aware of their reaction to your presence. If the birds become agitated or commence their *"tchip"* alarm calls, withdraw immediately to a less threatening distance. To avoid such conflicts, use binoculars and long camera lenses. These will allow you to observe and photograph ospreys without the need for being extremely close.

When approaching osprey colonies or nests, avoid the use of loud outboard motors, banging oars or paddles, and other foreign, startling sounds. Observe ospreys and their nests from a safe distance, and for short periods of time. There is no rule on how close you can get to individual ospreys, so experts suggest that you gauge each bird's reaction to your presence, and proceed accordingly.

Avoid direct contact with nests, platforms, poles and other nest structures. Do not climb into nests to handle eggs or young. Inexperienced osprey parents in particular may abandon a nest with young if your intrusion frightens or annoys them. Always put the welfare of your subject ahead of your own curiosity or interests. Remember, it has taken over thirty years to bring ospreys back to their present numbers, and every loss due to human intrusion is a step in the wrong direction.

Do not attempt to feed, handle or "rescue" injured ospreys you may encounter. Instead, call your state fish and wildlife department to report wounded or threatened birds, and make yourself available to the authorities for information or directions on where they can find you and the disabled birds or nests. These experts know what they are doing, and, in some cases, can even hatch eggs or fledge young retrieved from damaged nests. For example, in Boothbay, Maine, one osprey nest, built on the end of a pier, collapsed into the water during a storm—nest, chicks and all. The nest, still intact, was adrift and floating in the bay when biologists arrived to rescue the nestlings, which they hacked into other osprey nests and successfully fledged.

There is absolutely no reason ospreys should ever have to face the threat of extinction that occurred in the 1960s in the United States and elsewhere. Thanks to the dedication and hard work of unheralded researchers around the world, we now know what ospreys are and what they need to survive, and we know that they can exist, in harmony, with us. If we do our part, the ospreys will take care of the rest.

Following pages: Ospreys have recovered from the DDT scare of the1960s and are now the world's most common predatory bird.